ALLGÄU

Verlag: STUDIO TANNER   D-8964 Nesselwang

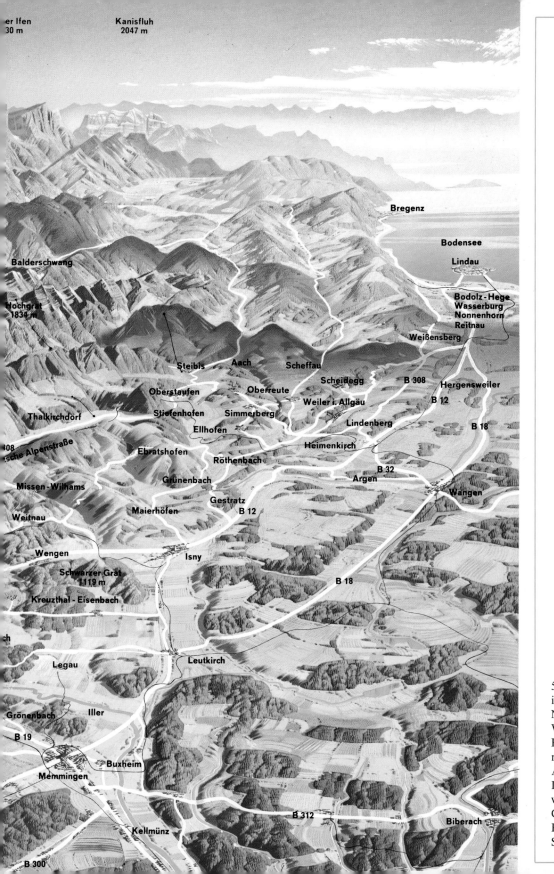

er Ifen
30 m

Kanisfluh
2047 m

Bregenz

Bodensee

Lindau

Balderschwang

Hochgrat
1834 m

Bodolz - Hege
Wasserburg
Nonnenhorn
Reitnau

Weißensberg

Steibis
Aach
Scheffau

Scheidegg

B 308

Hergensweiler

Oberstaufen
Oberreute

Weiler i. Allgäu

B 12

Thalkirchdorf
Stiefenhofen
Simmerberg

Lindenberg

B 18

Ellhofen

Heimenkirch

Ebratshofen
Röthenbach

che Alpenstraße
308

B 32

Missen - Wilhams
Grünenbach

Argen

Wangen

Gestratz

Weitnau
Maierhöfen
B 12

Wengen

Schwarzer Grät
1119 m

Isny

B 18

Kreuzthal - Eisenbach

Leutkirch

Legau

Grönenbach
Iller

B 19

Buxheim

Memmingen

B 312

Biberach

Kellmünz

B 300

5. Auflage erschienen 1979
im Verlag STUDIO TANNER D-8964 Nesselwang
Nachdruck, fotomechanische und sonstige
Wiedergabe, auch auszugsweise, ist nicht gestattet.
Reliefkarte: Heinrich Berann, Lans,
mit Genehmigung des Fremdenverkehrsverbandes
Allgäu/Bayerisch-Schwaben
Luftaufnahmen: freigegeben durch die Regierung
von Oberbayern Nr. G-24/2634, G-24/2624,
G-405/79, G-405/53. ISBN 3-9800066-0-3.
Fotos, Gestaltung und Gesamtherstellung:
STUDIO TANNER

Ein Land ohne feste politische Grenzen – eine Landschaft, so recht geschaffen zum Urlaubmachen – ein kleines Himmelreich für Fremde ebenso wie für Einheimische – das alles verbindet sich mit dem Begriff „Allgäu".

Sein Name ist so etwas wie ein Markenartikel mit Garantie für saftig grüne Wiesen, herrliche Naturseen, waldreiche Täler, für blumenübersäte Bergmatten und steil aufragende Felsgipfel. Man denkt an frische Milch, würzigen Käse, an einladende Dörfer und romantische Kleinstädte.

Nur Experten können die landschaftlichen Grenzen des Allgäus genau bestimmen. Im großen und ganzen erstreckt es sich in West-Ost-Richtung zwischen Bodensee und Lech. Im Nordwesten nimmt es ein Stückchen Württemberg in Anspruch und im Süden einige Täler und Gipfel aus Tirol und dem Vorarlbergischen. Nach Norden zu hört das Allgäu da auf, wo die Bergkette dem Blick langsam entschwindet. Womit nicht gesagt sein soll, daß das Allgäu an klaren Tagen nicht fast bis in die Gegend von Augsburg reichen kann.

Die gastfreundlichen Leute, die im Allgäu leben, sind bayerische Schwaben. Dennoch sind sie so echte

---

A region without fixed political boundaries; an ideal region for taking a holiday or having a good rest; a little paradise for outsiders as well as the local inhabitants – all this is conjured up by the word "Allgaeu".

The name "Allgaeu" stands for green fields, glorious natural lakes, wooded valleys, meadows strewn with flowers and mountain peaks rising steeply from their surroundings. It calls to mind fresh milk, spiced cheeses, delightful villages and romantic little towns.

Only the expert can pinpoint exactly the boundaries of the Allgaeu. From West to East the region lies roughly between Lake Constance and the River Lech. In the North-West it claims a bit of Wuerttemberg. In the South few valleys and mountains reach over into Tyrol and Vorarlberg. In the North the Allgaeu ends where the mountains gradually disappear from view, which doesn't mean to say that on a clear day you can see as far as Augsburg.

The hospitable people of the Allgaeu are Bavarian Swabians. However, this makes them as genuinely Swabians as any other Swabians. They are peaceloving, hard working, sincere and genuine. A people, not given to many words, they are patient almost to a fault but

---

Un pays sans frontière politique, un paysage comme «fait» pour se reposer, un petit paradis pour les touristes tout comme pour ceux qui y sont nés, voici l'Allgäu! Allgäu! N'est-ce pas là comme une garantie de verdure, des lacs naturels, de vallées ombragées bordées de pentes jonchées de fleurs et dominées par des sommets élevés? Et, ce seul nom n'évoque-t-il pas, tout à la fois, le souvenir de lait frais savoureux, de fromages onctueux, de villages rieurs et de petites cités romantiques?

Seuls des expert sauront définir avec précision les frontières naturelles de l'Allgäu. L'axe Ouest-Est est limité par le Lac de Constance à l'Ouest et la rivière Lech à l'Est. Le Nord-Est empiète quelque peu sur le Baden-Württemberg tandis qu'au Sud, vous trouverez plusieurs enclaves constituées par des vallées du Tyrol ou du Vorarlberg.

Vers le Nord, l'Allgäu prend fin là où les chaînes de montagnes s'estompent au loin. Ne vous y trompez pas cependant! Par temps clair, lorsque le ciel est dégagé, la vue s'étend pour ainsi dire jusqu'à Augsburg!

Sa population, que l'on dit très hospitalière, est composée de Souabes du Sud. Comme tout Souabe qui se respecte, le Souabe Bavarois aime sa tranquillité, travaille avec ardeur, se montre cordial

Schwaben wie alle anderen Schwaben auch: friedliebend, arbeitsam, herzlich und unverfälscht. In der Sprache nicht eben die redsamsten. Langmütig gewiß wie selten andere – und nur, wenn's wirklich sein muß, dazwischen auch einmal „saugrob".

Gar jede Jahreszeit im Allgäu hat ihre eigene Faszination. Wer wollte entscheiden, wann dieses Land am schönsten ist?
Zieht im Tal der Frühling ein mit seinen Krokuswiesen, locken am Nebelhorn gleißende Firnhänge und lassen das Skifahrerherz höher schlagen. Bald leckt die Sonne die letzten Schneeflecken von den Bergwiesen und hervor bricht eine unermeßliche Fülle von Bergblumen, eine Alpenflora, wie man sie anderswo kaum wiederfindet. Man meint, die Tage festhalten zu müssen, so schön sind sie.
Der Hochsommer im Allgäu wird nie zu heiß. Wo der leichte Bergwind nicht erfrischt, lädt ein idyllischer Moorsee zum Baden ein. Heu duftet auf den Wiesen und braungebrannte Gesichter lachen in den Tag.
In den Bergen ist der Sommer nicht lang. Unversehens liegt eines Morgens der Herbst in der Luft. September – Oktober sind Monate für Genießer. Die Luft wird dünn

when provoked they are not mincing words, they are as one says "saugrob".
The Allgaeu is attractive in every season of the year. Who would really want to decide when this region is at its best?
When Spring comes to the valleys with meadows full of crocuses, glistening permanent snow beckons from the peak of the Nebelhorn and puts joy into every skier's heart. But it is not long before the sun melts away the last patches of snow from the mountain pastures and coaxes out endless varieties of mountain and Alpine flowers, spreading a rich carpet, the like of which you will find hardly anywhere else. Each passing day is so bright, you want to hold it fast.
In mid-Summer the Allgaeu is never too hot. If there is no mountain breeze to refresh you, there is bound to be an idyllic moorland lake inviting you to swim.
The scent of hay is everywhere and smiling brown faces greet the day.
Summer is short in the mountains. Suddenly one morning there is an Autumn nip in the air. September and October are months for the connoisseur. The air is thin and as clear as a bell, the mountain peaks seem so close that you could almost touch them and

s'avérant, avant tout, d'un grand naturel. Il n'est pas très bavard, lent à se mettre en colère, . . . rustre à souhait cependant lorsque son tempérament l'emporte.
Chaque saison s'accompagne de sa propre fascination. Définir la plus belle s'avère tâche bien difficile!
Lorsque le printemps fait son entrée dans la vallée et que les prés se couvrent de crocus, le Hochgrat et le Nebelhorn encore tout enneigés sont le paradis des skieurs. Bientôt, le soleil fait fondre les dernières langues de neige et, c'est alors, l'épanouissement de cette multitude de fleurs, flore alpestre inoubliable et jamais égalée. Que ne peut-on, alors, retenir le temps et fixer à jamais la beauté de ces journées . . .
L'été est toujours agréable à la montagne. Une brise légère vient tempérer les grosses chaleurs de midi; là, un lac perdu dans la nature invite aux joies de la baignade. Une odeur de foin coupé flotte dans l'air – des visages bronzés vous sourient.
Bientôt, c'est l'automne. Les amoureux de la nature apprécieront les mois de Septembre et d'Octobre lorsque l'air se transforme et que l'on croit pourvoir, subitement, toucher du doigt les sommets environnants qui semblent tout proches. Le Bergahorn revêt sa lumineuse parure d'automne. C'est le temps idéal

„Getreu dem guten alten Brauch". Historische Trachtengruppe, Oberstdorf.

Faithful to the good old ways – an Oberstdorf group in traditional costume.

Fidélitè aux anciennes traditions – groupe folklorique à Oberstdorf.

und glasklar, die Gipfel rücken zum Greifen nahe und der Bergahorn leuchtet in herbstlicher Farbenpracht. Allerorts hört man das Glockengeläut der Viehherden beim Alpabtrieb. Jetzt ist das Wetter sicher für den „Heilbronner Weg", den berühmten Felsenweg über den Allgäuer Hauptkamm vom Hohen Licht zur Mädelegabel.
Wenn das Jahr zur Neige geht, fallen für kurze Zeit die Nebel ins Tal. Und schon werden sie freudig begrüßt wie gute Bekannte: die ersten tanzenden Schneeflocken am Fenster. Über Nacht hüllen sie Berge und Täler in ihr winterliches Kleid. Über Nacht hat das Allgäu ein neues Gesicht: blauer Winterhimmel, Schlittenfahrt zur Wildfütterung, abends Glühwein am Kamin, Skibetrieb auf Pisten oder leichtes Gleiten auf stillen Skiwanderwegen.
Dieses Land, das Allgäu heißt, ist immer aufs neue unbeschreiblich schön. Besser als Worte sollen es die folgenden Bilder zeigen. Und noch besser ist es, selbst zu schauen und das zu erleben, was Worte und Bilder nicht zeigen können.

everything around glows in its Autumn colours. This is the sign that the weather is settled enough to take the "Heilbronn path", the famous rocky climb over the mountains from Hohes Licht to Maedelegabel. All around you will hear cow bells as the stock is herded down from the mountain alms.
When the year draws to its close, there is only a short season of mists in the valleys. Very soon you find yourself being welcomed like an old friend by the first snowflakes dancing past your window. Over night the mountains and valleys put on their winter attire, and the Allgaeu appears in a new and different beauty.
This means blue Winter sky, sleigh-rides to feed the deer, evenings at the fireside, drinking mulled wine and days spent skiing down the runs or just ski-rambling along quiet trails.
This region known as the Allgaeu is indescribably beautiful all year round, for which the following photographs will vouch more eloquently than words. But the best way to find out is to come and see, and experience for yourself, what neither words nor pictures can convey.

pour s'attaquer à la classique route des crêtes reliant le Hohen Licht à la Mädelegabel. Des quatre coins de l'horizon retentissent les tintements joyeux des clochettes accompagnant la descente des troupeaux. Lorsque l'année touche à sa fin, le brouillard s'installe dans la vallée. Puis, apparaissent les premiers flocons. Ils dansent et tourbillonnent devant la fenêtre et ici, dans la montagne, on les accueille comme de vieux amis. Le temps d'une nuit, les montagnes et les vallées se parent de leur blanc manteau d'hiver.
Visage nouveau de l'Allgäu: ciel bleu d'hiver, courses en traineaux vers les refuges où les animaux de la forêt, chassés par le froid, viennent se nourrir; ce sont aussi les joies du ski sur les pentes neigeuses tout autant, d'ailleurs, que celles de l'aprés-ski qui réunit jeunes et moins jeunes au coin de l'âtre! Pour celui qui aime la nature et la montagne, nul n'est besoin de répéter combien l'Allgäu est beau tout au long des saisons qui passent. Mieux que des mots, les photos réunies dans cet album vont vous le prouver et vous inviter à découvrir par vous-même ce coin de la Bavière cher à notre cœur que nous aimerions, ainsi, vous faire connaître.

„Schrothgekurt ist neu geboren". Das ist seit 1950 Wahlspruch in Oberstaufen, dem einzigen Schrothkurort Deutschlands. Ganzjähriger Kurbetrieb und eine große Tradition als Wintersportplatz gehören zum Erfolgsrezept der Kurverwaltung. Und dazu noch zwei Olympia-Siegerinnen: Heidi Biebl, die waschechte Oberstaufenerin, und Christl Cranz-Borchers in ihrer Wahlheimat Steibis.

Since 1950 the motto of Oberstaufen has been that a "Schroth-cure" is as good as being reborn. This is the only health resort in Germany run on Schroth-principles. Part of the town's success is due to the fact that the cures can be taken all year round and that it has an established reputation as a winter sportcentre. Both aspects are the responsibility of a special municipal department. To this may be added that it is the home of two Olympic-Gold-Winners: Heidi Biebl, a native of Oberstaufen, and Christl Cranz-Borchers who has settled in Steibis.

Oberstaufen et ses fameuses cures de blé égurgé au sortir desquelles l'on se sent comme renaître! Ville de cures, centre sportif, Oberstaufen compte parmi ses citadins les plus cèlèbres: Heidi Biebl et Christl Cranz-Borchers.

Zwar etwas abseits, aber für Kenner so etwas wie ein Geheimtip: Steibis, die Sonnenterrasse hoch über dem Weißachtal.

The sun terrace at Steibis high above the valley of the Weissach – slightly off the beaten track and something of a secret passed on among connoisseurs.

Située à l'écart, à l'usage exclusif des connaisseurs, voici Steibis, terrasse ensoleillée dominant la vallée de Weissach.

Der Hochgrat – Kulminationspunkt und Aussichtskanzel der Allgäuer Nagelfluhkette – läßt sich mit den schmucken gelben Gondeln der Hochgratbahn mühelos „ersteigen". An klaren Tagen reicht der Blick von den Schweizer Gletschern bis zu Deutschlands höchstem Gipfel, der Zugspitze.

The Hochgrat – summit of the „Nagelfluh"-mountains. The yellow cabins of a funicular carry you with ease to the top, saving you the efforts of a hard climb.

Le Hochgrat – point culminant de la «chaine Nagelfluh» de l'Allgäu – les pimpantes gondoles jaunes du téléphérique du Hochgrat vous permettront de «l'escalader» facilement.

Immenstadt, von den Einheimischen liebevoll „s'Städtle" genannt, ist mit seiner 600jährigen Geschichte Mittelpunkt des wirtschaftlichen und kulturellen Lebens.

Immenstadt – „our little town" as the natives call it endearingly – is by its 600 years old history and tradition a cultural as well as economic center.

Immenstadt, que ses citadins appellant amoureusement «le petit bourg» s'appuie sur le poids de ses 600 ans d'histoire pour faire face à ses activités de centre économique et culturel.

Sommer, Sonne, Segeln – die „Erholungslandschaft Großer Alpsee" ist ein Paradies für Wasserratten, Wellensegler und Wanderer. Von ganz oben, von den Almen und Gipfeln, blickt man in ein wiesengrünes und wasserblaues Bilderbuch.

The recreational area of „Grosser Alpsee" is a veritable paradise for all loving summer, sun, mountains and water. Its lakes invite to all sorts of aquatic sports. From mountain peaks or high up pastures a dazzling view of almost unreal beauty rewards the hiker feasting his eyes on the blue of lakes and the fresh green of meadows.

Eté – soleil – faire voile – «le centre de repos le grand Alpsee» est un paradis pour les fanatiques de l'eau et les passionnés de la voile, tout comme pour les amateurs de longues promenades. Du haut des pâturages et des sommets, on découvre un vèritable paysage de livre d'images, avec le vert de ses prairies et le bleu des lacs.

Sonthofen – Tor zu den Tälern des oberen Allgäus – ist nicht nur wirtschaftlicher Mittelpunkt; seit 1973 ist die rührige Stadt auch Verwaltungssitz des neu gebildeten Landkreises Oberallgäu.

Sonthofen, the gateway to the valleys of the upper Allgaeu, is not merely a commercial centre. Since 1973 this bustling town has been the headquarters of the recently constituted administrative district of Oberallgaeu.

Sonthofen – porte ouverte sur la vallée de l'Allgäu. Centre économique, centre administratif aussi depuis la réorganisation de la région du Haut-Allgäu en 1973.

Weit schweift der Blick von den Hängen des Grünten über Burgberg in den wiesengrünen Kessel des Illertals bis zur prächtigen Kulisse des Allgäuer Hauptkamms.

From the slopes of the Gruenten-peak the eye can travel past Burgberg to the basin of the Iller-valley with its green fields, and on to the magnificent main-ridge of the Allgaeu-mountains.

Panorama impressionnant qui englobe les pentes du Grünten dominant Burgberg et la vallée verdoyante de l'Iller avec, en arrière-plan, les principaux sommets de l'Allgäu.

Ofterschwang – Oase der Ruhe zwischen
heuduftenden Wiesen und schattenspendenden
Wäldern.

Ofterschwang is a quiet oasis surrounded by
hay-scented meadows and shady woods.

Ofterschwang – oasis de calme et de verdure.

Die Sonnenalp – ein Haus voller gastlicher
Traditionen – ist so etwas wie ein Aushängeschild
der Allgäuer Gastronomie. Von einer Familie in
landschaftsgebundenem Stil erbaut, mit viel Liebe
zum Detail und freundlichem, persönlichem
Service.

The Sonnenalp, a hotel with a tradition of hospitality,
is true a standard for gastronomy in the Allgaeu.
It is built in a style harmonising with its surroundings,
and run with loving care and guarantees friendly and
personal service.

Sonnenalp (alpage du soleil) – la Maison se présente
àvous avec sa tradition gastronomique, le charme de
son architecture et son accueil chaleureux.

Nicht nur in Schöllang – „Vorfahrt für Kühe!" Wer kennt nicht diese ungeschriebene Allgäuer Verkehrsordnung? Die ländliche Idylle und der Blick übers Tal auf Fischen ist etwas für geruhsame PS-Genießer.

"Cows have right of way" – not only in Schoellang! Who hasn't come across this unwritten rule of the Allgaeu highwaycode?
This rural idyll and the view over the valley to Fischen are only for unhurried motorists.

A Schöllang, comme partout ailleurs, «priorité aux ruminants!» Connaissiez-vous ce complément au code de la route?
L'automobiliste flâneur se plaira à goûter, ainsi, les charmes particuliers du paysage.
Vue sur Fischen.

Nebelhorn, Rubihorn und deren Hörner mehr auf der anderen Talseite blicken felsig oder
bewaldet auf liebliche Feriendörfer.
Fischen ist Sitz der neugebildeten Verwaltungsgemeinschaft „Hörnergruppe". Hier findet der Gast
eine breitgefächerte Urlaubspalette vom beheizten Freischwimmbad bis zum „Fiskina"-Kursaal.

Nebelhorn, Rubihorn and many other rocky or wooded peaks look down from the far side of the
valley on villages which are delightful holiday bases.
Fischen is not simply the headquarters of the recently established administrative district of
Hoernergruppe. Here the visitor will find a wide-ranging choice of holiday facilities from the
heated open air swimmingpool to the "Fiskina" centre.

Nebelhorn, Rubihorn dominent maints villages et hameaux souriants dont Fischen aux
multiples possibilités de détente.

Für Einheimische und Gäste das Ereignis des Sommers:
Alpabtrieb in Balderschwang.
Heute durch den Riedbergpaß erschlossen, war Balderschwang noch in
den 50er Jahren eines der abgelegensten Allgäuer Hochtäler.

Herding cattle down from the alms in Balderschwang – this is the most
important event of the Summer for both natives and visitors. Whilst
Balderschwang has now been made accessible via the Riedberg pass,
this area, as recently as the 1950's, was still one of the most secluded,
and proverbially arctic, of the high valleys of the Allgaeu.

Pour les touristes – tout autant que pour ceux qui y sont nés –, une
attraction particulière : la descente des troupeaux des alpages.
Il y a 20 ans encore, Balderschwang ressemblait à un village sibérien,
isolé du reste du monde. Aujourd'hui le Col du Riedberg en facilite
l'accès.

Klirrender Winter in Obermaiselstein. ▶
Von hier verbindet Deutschlands höchster Alpenpaß das Balderschwanger
Tal mit der Oberallgäuer Außenwelt.

Crisp Winter in Obermaiselstein. This is the starting point of the
Riedberg pass road which connects the valley of Balderschwang with the
rest of the Allgaeu beyond the peaks.

Hiver très rude dans l'Obermaiselstein. Le col du Riedberg relie la
vallée de Balderschwang à l'arrière pays.

Oberstdorf – „oberstes Dorf" im Illertal und Allgäuer
Fremdenverkehrsmetropole – „par excellence".
Heilklimatischer Kurort mit jener glücklichen Mischung von Eleganz
und Komfort, bodenständiger Dörflichkeit und etwas Snobismus, die die
unaufdringliche Atmosphäre eines internationalen Ferienplatzes ausmacht.

Oberstdorf (meaning "highest village") in the Iller-valley is the most
famous touristcentre in the Allgaeu. It is a healthresort where visitors
come for the clean, healthy air. It combines elegance and comfort as well
as the atmosphere of villagelife. It is in the true sense an international
holidayresort.

Oberstdorf (traduit litéralement «village le plus élevé») dans la vallée de
l'Iller. Centre touristique par excellence (en Français dans le texte).
Synonyme de comfort et d'élégance. Contraste entre son caractère
rustical et sa fidélité aux traditions et un certain snobisme propre aux grands
centres internationaux de tourisme.

Das Sommerdorf Gerstruben – vermutlich die älteste Allgäuer Siedlung –
hat noch nichts von seiner ursprünglichen Ruhe und Beschaulichkeit
eingebüßt.

The summer village of Gerstruben, thought to be the oldest settlement
in the Allgaeu, has not yet sacrificed any of its tranquility.

Gerstruben – à beaucoup d'égards, la cité la plus ancienne de l'Allgäu,
n'a rien perdu de son calme légendaire et de son pittoresque. ▶

Vorbei am blauen Spiegel des Freibergsees führt der Wanderweg ins herbstliche Birgsautal. Bergpfade leiten von Einödsbach über Grasmatten zu den sommerwarmen Felsen der Trettach und zum Kreuz an der Rappenseehütte. Hier beginnt der berühmte „Heilbronner Weg", ein Felsensteig für Schwindelfreie über die höchsten Allgäuer Gipfel vom Hohen Licht bis zur Mädelegabel.

The path leads past the calm blue water of Freiberg-lake and along the Birgsau-valley, her you see it in its Autumncolours. Mountain-paths lead on from Einoedsbach across highland-pastures to the rocks of the Trettach or to the cross near the Rappen-lake-hut. This is the beginning of the famous Heilbronn-trail, a rocky climb only for experienced Alpinists. The path leads from Hohes Licht to Maedelegabel, the highest peaks of the Allgaeu.

Avec le bleu particulier de ses eaux, voici le lac Freiberg, point de départ d'une admirable promenade qui mène dans la vallée du Birgsau. Par delà des sentiers étroits et des prairies à l'herbe drue, c'est la découverte des rochers du Trettach et de la fameuse croix au pied du refuge du Rappensee. C'est ici que commence le «Chemin de Heilbronn», véritable «route des crêtes» rocailleuse réservée à ceux qui ne craignent pas le vertige, reliant ainsi les sommets les plus élevés de l'Allgäu, du Hohen Licht à la Mädelegabel.

Höher als der Eiffelturm: eindrucksvolle 189 Meter erhebt sich der Anlaufturm der Skiflugschanze über dem Birgsautal.
Steckbrief 1973: Weltrekord Wosipiwo – DDR, 169 m

Higher than the Eiffel Tower – the inrun tower for the skiflying ramp rises an impressive 189 metres above the Birgsau valley.
1973 success: a world record of 169 m by Wosipiwo, DDR

Plus haut que la Tour Eiffel! Tremplin de saut en longueur dominant la vallée de la Birgsau.
1973: record mondial détenu par Wosipiwo (DDR) avec un saut de 169 m.

Strahlender Wintertag über Tiefenbach und seinen Bergen.

White caps have settled on the starlings' nesting boxes: Deepest Winter reigns over Tiefenbach and its peaks.

Bonnets blancs pour les maisons de Tiefenbach. L'hiver a fait son entrée.

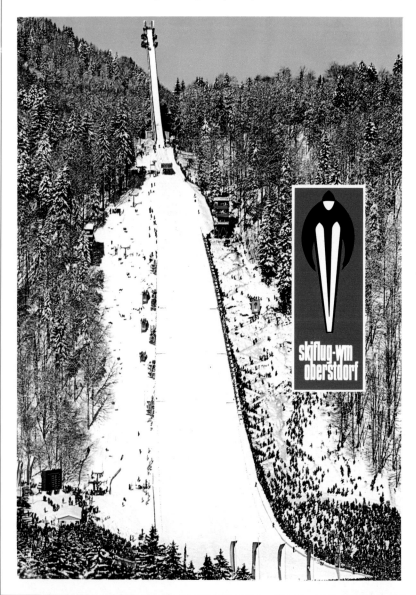

Schwerelos in die Bläue des Allgäuer Berghimmels:
Die Nebelhornbahn hat oben noch einen Umsteiger. Per Sessellift geht's zur Aussichtsterrasse
am Gipfelhaus.

An easy way up to the blue sky above the Allgaeu-mountains:
The Nebelhorn funicular continues by chairlift up to the peak with its glorious view.

Vue panoramique des sommets de l'Allgäu du haut de la cabine du téléphérique du Nebelhorn,
prolongé par un télésiège donnant accès à la terrasse aménagée au sommet de la montagne.

Laurins Rosengarten in voller Blüte:
Im Kleinen Walsertal (gehört zu Vorarlberg mit
Haustür im Allgäu) entwickelt die Alpenflora ihre
üppige Pracht, besonders zur Alpenrosenzeit.

The legendary King Laurin's Rose-Garden in full
bloom;
in the lower Walser-valley (which belongs to
Vorarlberg but has its front door, so to speak, in the
Allgaeu) the Alpine flora puts on a luxuriant
display, particularly when the Alpine-Roses are in
bloom.

Un régal pour l'œil. Dans le petit Walsertal
(appartenant au Vorarlberg avec une porte ouverte
sur l'Allgäu), c'est la profusion extraordinaire des
roses des Alpes s'épanouissant au cœur de la nature.

Wo einst die Salzfrächter mühsam übers
unwirtliche Joch zogen, verbringt man heute Ferien
mit Komfort: Oberjoch mit seinem Hausberg,
dem 1876 m hohen Iseler.

Oberjoch and its 1876 metre high peak, the Iseler;
salt carriers once toiled over this inhospitable pass
but now holiday-makers spend their days in comfort.

L'ancienne route du sel et ses hameaux présentent
aujourd'hui toutes les caractéristiques d'un centre de
tourisme moderne, dominé par l'Iseler (1876 m
d'altitude).

Dörfliche Idylle und gleichzeitig moderner Kurort:
In Hindelang-Bad Oberdorf wurde beides in selten
glücklicher Harmonie vereint.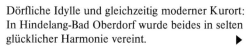

Hindelang-Bad Oberdorf is a rare combination of
both, village idyll and modern healthresort.

Romantisme et charme surrané s'harmonisent avec
le modernisme des stations balnéaires 'voici
Hindelang-Bad Oberdorf.

Sankt Hubertus ist der Schutzpatron der kleinen
Kapelle im Hintersteiner Tal.

St. Hubert is the patron saint of this little chapel in
the Hinterstein-valley.

Petite chapelle dans la vallée de Hinterstein dédiée
à St. Hubert.

Folklore nicht nur für Kurgäste:
Die Pflege altüberlieferten Brauchtums, historischer Trachten und Feste ist ein echtes Anliegen
der heimatverbundenen Bewohner des Ostrachtals.

Folklore is not only for visitors –
the inhabitants of the Ostrach-valley, closely bound to their native soil, are genuinely interested
in preserving historical costumes and festivals and keeping up customs handed down from
the past.

Maintient des traditions folkloriques, des costumes locaux et des fêtes villageoises chères au
cœur des habitants de la vallée de l'Ostrach.

Luftaufnahme von Bad Oberdorf?
Zu Recht trägt dieser „luftige" Aussichtsplatz an der Jochpaßstraße den Namen „Kanzel".

Aerial view of Bad Oberdorf?
This airy vantage point on the pass road is appropriately called the "pulpit".

Bad Oberdorf à vol d'oiseau.

In Hinterstein endet die Straße für PS-Ausflügler. Weiter talein kommt nur noch, wer auf Schusters Rappen die Abgeschiedenheit des Tals genießen will.

Hinterstein is the end of the road for motorists. Only those who are content to make do on Shanks' pony may continue up the valley and enjoy its seclusion.

Hinterstein, «tout le monde descend»! Pour découvrir la vallée et goûter son calme, l'on poursuit son chemin à pied!

Pistenglück und Wedelfreuden am Grünten.
Rings um Kranzegg erschließen ein rundes Dutzend
Lifte und Bahnen die schneesicheren Hänge bis
hinauf zum aussichtsreichen Gipfel.

The joys of ski runs and "wedeln" down the Gruenten.
A good dozen chair lifts and a funicular near
Kranzegg take you up to slopes, where snow can be
guaranteed.

Joies du ski sur les pentes du Grünten. Tout autour
de Kranzegg, une douzaine de remonte-pentes et de
téléphériques donnent accès aux pistes aménagées
sur les hauts plateaux.

Nicht jeder hat das Glück, einen ausgewachsenen
Zwölfender am Futterplatz zu sehen. Nur die
intensive Fütterung der Jäger hilft den Tieren durch
den harten Bergwinter.

Not everyone is lucky enough to see a full grown
stag with twelve points at the feeding place. Only
intensive feeding by the rangers keeps the animals
alive through a hard winter in the mountains.

Quelle aubaine que de rencontrer un cerf pareil.
Grâce aux soins attentifs des chasseurs, nos amis de
la forêt peuvent faire face aux rigueurs de l'hiver.

„Wo das Alphorn tönt . . ."
Sonntagmorgen auf taufrischen Wiesen über
Rettenberg.

Where the Alpine horn is heard –
meadows wet with dew on a Sunday morning above
Rettenberg.

L'appel du cor alpestre vient briser le calme du
matin dans les près innondés de rosée au-dessus du
Rettenberg.

Leute, die es wissen müssen, nennen sie die älteste Stadt Deutschlands:
Aus dem „Campodunum" der alten Römer erwuchs Kempten, die freundliche Metropole des
Allgäus. Modern, aufgeschlossen und dennoch mit einer reizvollen Altstadt voller Romantik.

Those, who should know, call this the oldest town of Germany. The "Campodunum" of the
Roman times became Kempten, the friendly metropolis of the Allgaeu. In many ways modernized,
it still has a very charming, romantic old centre.

On l'appelle la ville la plus ancienne d'Allemagne. C'est Kempten, issue du «Campodunum» des
Romains, métropole souriante de l'Allgäu. Cité moderne et dynamique, elle a su préserver une
partie de son caractère romantique.

Eine Landschaft zum Verlieben: das Allgäuer Voralpenland mit seinen Wiesen, Wäldern, Bergen und Seen.
Blick vom Blender auf Buchenberg (oben).
Niedersonthofener See (unten).
Grüntensee (rechts).

A bit of the Lower Alps which are part of the Allgaeu – you can hardly fail to fall in love with its meadows, woods, mountains and lakes.
View from the Blender to Buchenberg (above).
Niedersonthofen-lake (below).
Gruenten-lake (right).

Comment résister au coup de foudre pour ce merveilleux paysage? Voici la campagne de l'Allgäu avec ses prairies verdoyantes, ses forêts ombrageuses, ses montagnes et ses lacs.
Vue du Blender sur Buchenberg (en haut).
Lac de Niedersonthofen (en bas).
Lac de Grünten (à droite).

Dort, wo sich der Blick auf Säuling und Zugspitze auftut, beginnt das Ostallgäuer Land.
Der Kneipp-Kurort Oy erfreut sich Sommer wie Winter großer Beliebtheit.

Where the eye sweeps upwards to the Saeuling and the Zugspitze there begins the Eastern Allgaeu. The healthresort of Oy, run on Kneipp principles, is popular in Winter as well as in Summer.

Découverte du Säuling et de la Zugspitze en arrièreplan. Oy – station thermale fidèle aux principes de Kneipp.

1036 Meter hoch liegt Mittelberg auf der Sonnenterrasse über Grüntensee und Wertachtal.

Mittelberg, at an altitude of 1036 metres, lies on the sunny plateau above Gruenten-lake and Wertach-valley.

À 1036 m d'altitude, voici Mittelberg, terrasse ensoleillée dominant le Grüntensee et la vallée de Wertach.

Weithin sichtbar, markant und eindrucksvoll erhebt sich der Grünten –
der „Wächter des Allgäus" – über Wertach, dem höchstgelegenen
deutschen Marktflecken.

Known as the guardian of the Allgaeu and visible for miles, the
characteristic massif of the Gruenten rises impressively above Wertach,
the highest German market town.

Wertach, au pied du Grünten que l'on appelle aussi «le gardien de
l'Allgäu».

Wenige Kilometer talauf dauert der Winter von Dezember bis April.
Unterjoch kennt keine Schneesorgen.

Only a few miles further on, Winter lasts from December to April.
Unterjoch never has to worry about having enough snow.

Unterjoch, paradis des skieurs, du mois de decembre au mois d'avril.

Verwöhnen lassen bei Sachertorte und Kaffeeduft
kann man sich auf der Sonnenterrasse des
Kur- und Sporthotels Tirol.

You can treat yourself to coffee and cake on the
Hotel Tyrol's sunterrace which caters to both
visitors taking a cure and those who come for
winter sports.

Farniente sur la terrasse du Sporthotel Tyrol fier de
sa vielle tradition gastronomique.

Jungholz – ein kleines Stück Österreich zwischen
Allgäuer Bergen – darf auf die Leistungen seiner
Gastronomie stolz sein.

Jungholz, a little patch of Austria trapped between
the mountains of the Allgaeu, has a gastronomic
reputation of which it is justly proud.

Jungholz – petite enclave autrichienne dans les
montagnes de l'Allgäu.

Nesselwang, bekannt als „Skidorf des Allgäus", ist auch im Sommer ein vielbesuchtes
Ferienziel mit blitzsauberen Häusern, idyllischen Seen und gastfreundlichen Leuten.
Wer wollte sich hier nicht schon am ersten Tag zu Hause fühlen?

Nesselwang is known as "the Allgaeu skiing village". With its bright clean houses,
enchanting lakes and hospitable inhabitants it is also much visited in Summer. Who wouldn't
feel at home here from the first?

Nesselwang – village de skieurs en hiver par excellence, c'est aussi, en été, une adorable petite
commune aux maisons pimpantes et riantes.

Mit dem Lift fast bis zur Haustür oder zu Fuß
zwei abwechslungsreiche Stunden Aufstieg:
Die Einkehr im Sportheim Böck lohnt sich in jedem
Fall.

Take a chairlift almost to the front door, or follow
the footpath, which means a two-hour climb through
varied scenery; whichever way, you chose, the
Sportheim Böck is worth a visit.

Où irez-vous en promenade? Chez Böck, le
restaurants des sportifs dont les plus authentiques
accepteront volontiers l'idée d'une marche de deux
heures environ! Pour les paresseux, un télésiège les
y déposera.

Einer der vielgeliebten Allgäuer Moorseen:
der Attlesee bei Nesselwang.

One of the Allgaeu's very popular moorland lakes –
the Attlesee near Nesselwang.

Attlesee près de Nesselwang.

Liebhaber nennen es „die Perle des Allgäus", das Pfrontener Tal mit seinen dreizehn Ortsteilen, die alle den gleiche Vornamen „Pfronten" tragen. Wahrzeichen des Tals ist der schlanke, barocke Turm der Pfarrkirche St. Nikolaus.

Those who have "discovered" it, call it the pearl of the Allgaeu. This is the valley of Pfronten with its thirteen parishes each of which prefixes "Pfronten" to its name. The landmark of the valley is the slim baroque steeple of the parish church of St. Nicholas. Its roof was inspired by a Gentian turned upside down.

Ses amoureux l'appellent «la perle de l'Allgäu» – Voici la vallée de Pfronten avec ses 13 villages pittoresques et sa magnifique église baroque St. Nicolas dont le clocher au toit taillé en forme de gentiane, s'élance vers le ciel.

Von schwerer Last gebeugt:
Bergföhren an der Baumgrenze trotzen dem
langen Winter am Aggenstein.

Weighed down by their burden, mountain pines at
the forest line defy the long Winter on the
Aggenstein.

Ils croulent sous le poid de leur lourde charge!
Espèce particulière de pins poussant sur les pentes
de l'Aggenstein.

Badesaison auch im Winter:
Am Meilinger Hang oberhalb der kleinen Kapelle
entstand das neue Sport- und Erholungszentrum mit
Freischwimmbecken und Hallenbad und einem
prächtigen Panoramablick auf das Tal und seine
Berge.

In Pfronten the swimming season continues
throughout the Winter as well. A new sports and
recuperation centre with open air and covered
swimmingpools and a magnificent panoramic view
of the valley and its peaks has been built on the
slopes of Meilingen above the little chapel.

Centre sportif inauguré en 1973, niché au flanc de la
montagne avec piscine, pistes de bowling,
bibliothèque, restaurant, voici la dernière corde que
Pfronten vient d'ajouter à son arc!

Blumenüberrankt, breit und behäbig, als sei er in die Landschaft gewachsen: der Berggasthof auf der Schloßanger Alp.
Darüber erhebt sich stolz, mit schwindelerregendem Talblick, Deutschlands höchstgelegene Burgruine
Falkenstein (1286 m).
Kurz unter dem Gipfel die mächtige Felsengrotte mit liebevoll gepflegtem Blumenschmuck.

Standing four square and covered with flowering creepers, the mountain restaurant on the Schlossanger-Alp looks
almost as though it had grown out of its surroundings.
Above rises the ruin of Falkenstein-Castle with its breathtaking view of the valley far below. At an altitude of 1286 m
this is the highest castle ruin anywhere in Germany.
Just below the peak there is a huge rock grotto with carefully tended flowers.

Couvert de fleurs, à l'architecture imposante, l'hôtel Schloßanger Alp semble faire corps avec le paysage.
A l'arrière plan s'élève la ruine du Falkenstein (1286 m).

Freundliche rote Gondeln schweben mit fröhlichen Insassen bergan und talab.
Die Breitenbergbahn führt von Pfronten-Steinach zur Hochalpe. Von hier kann die 1838 m hoch gelegene Ostlerhütte
teils per Sessellift, teils munter zu Fuß erreicht werden.

Cheerful red cabins float upwards with their passengers, and then back to the valley.
The Breitenberg funicular goes from Pfronten-Steinach to the Hochalpe. From there it is possible to continue,
partly by chairlift and partly on foot, to the 1838 m high Ostlerhütte on the Breitenberg-peak.

Gondoles rouges du téléphériques reliant Pfronten et le Breitenberg avec son refuge situé à 1838 m d'altitude.

Wenn Gemsen Glocken tragen, sind's meist Bergziegen – wie hier am Aggenstein.

If the chamois, you saw, was wearing a bell, it was certainly a mountain goat, as is the case here on the Aggenstein.

Lorsque les «chamois» portent des clochettes autour du cou, ce sont, en règle générale, de simples chevrettes! Nous les voyons ici sur les pentes de l'Aggenstein.

Alphornklänge über dem Tal gehören zu den eindrucksvollen Erinnerungen an einen wohlgelungenen Pfronten-Urlaub.

The sound of the Alpine horn floating down to the valley is one of the most unforgettable memories of a satisfactory holiday in Pfronten.

L'appel du cor!

Strandpromenade, Kaffee-Terrassen und Kurhotels,
weiße Segelboote und hübsche Badenixen.
Das ist die Atmosphäre, die Hopfen am See als
„Riviera des Allgäus" bekanntgemacht hat.

A lakeside walk, coffee terraces and healthresort-
hotels, boats with white sails and pretty girls in
bathing suits – this is the ambience that has given
Hopfen am See its reputation as the "Allgaeu's
Riviera".

Hopfen – Riviera de l'Allgäu avec sa promenade,
ses hôtels er ses voiliers blancs.

Wer's etwas ruhiger liebt, sollte Seeg als
Urlaubsdomizil wählen. Die abwechslungsreiche
Landschaft mit ihren verträumten Moor- und
Badeseen macht die Umgebung als Ferienparadies
ausgesprochen attraktiv.

For those who prefer really quiet surroundings, Seeg
is a good choice as a holiday base. The interesting
countryside with its moorland and lakes for
swimming makes this area a particularly attractive
holiday paradise.

Pour ceux qui préfèrent la calme, voici Seeg.

Malerische Gassen, das ehemalige Kloster St. Mang und die Abteikirche des Johann Jakob Herkomer ziehen Besucher aus aller Herren Ländern ebenso an wie der tosende Lechfall mit seinem blankgetretenen Stein, dem legendären „Magnustritt". Hoch über der Stadt das ehemalige Schloß der Fürstbischöfe von Augsburg, die von 1322 bis 1803 Herren von Füssen waren.

Picturesque narrow streets, the former monastery of St. Mang and Johann Jakob Herkomer's abbey-church are hardly less attractive to the many visitors from all over the world than the rushing Lech-waterfall. High above the town is situated the former palace of the prince bishops of Augsburg, who have been the sovereigns of Fuessen from 1322 to 1803.

Des ruelles étroites et pittoresques, l'ancienne abbaye de St. Mang et l'église de Jean-Jacques Herkomer ainsi que les chutes du Lech dominées par l'imposante statue de Magnus sont les points d'attraction de Füssen, tout autant que le vieux château, siège des Princes-Evêques d'Augsburg, maîtres incontestés de la région de 1322 à 1803.

Schloß Neuschwanstein – Märchenschloß des Bayernkönigs Ludwig II. – erhebt sich auf steilem Fels über der
Pöllat-Schlucht, die den schönsten, wenn auch beschwerlichsten Aufstieg zum Schloß bildet.
Wer hier einmal im Mondlicht die Freitreppen zum Schloßkonzert emporgestiegen ist, ahnt etwas vom Zauber,
der von diesem Bauwerk über alle Welt ausgeht.

The castle of Neuschwanstein, the fairytale castle of the Bavarian King, Ludwig II, rises from the steep rocks,
overhanging the Poellat ravine, which provides the most beautiful approach to the castle.
Anyone who climbs the open stairs on a moonlight night on his way to a concert in the castle, senses something of the
magic, which radiates from this edifice to the four corners of the earth.

Château de Neuschwanstein – véritable féerie, édifiée sur le désir du Roi de Bavière Louis II, se dressant sur les
rochers qui surplombent les gorges de Pöllat.
Il faut avoir goûté l'enchantement particulier dégagé par le château les soirs de concert donnés en été,
lors de la belle saison.

Bescheidener als sein prunkvoller Nachbar:
das Schloß Hohenschwangau im schlicht-vornehmen Stil ist dennoch (oder gerade deshalb)
einen Besuch wert.

More modest than its magnificent neighbour, the simple but elegant castle of Hohenschwangau
is nonetheless (or perhaps for this very reason) worth a visit.

Un peu plus loin, c'est le château de Hohenschwangau au charme plus discret mais non moins
évident.

Schwangauer Kleinod am Feldweg:
das Kirchlein St. Koloman, kunsthistorisch wie
landschaftlich gleichermaßen reizvoll.

A veritable jewel in the midst of green fields in
the "Schwangau district" is the little church of
St. Koloman, attractive both in its setting and from
an artistic point of view.

Petite curiosité historique en bordure de chemin,
c'est la petite chapelle de St. Coloman.

Tiefes Himmelsblau spiegelt sich im Forggensee.
Das ist die Zeit der Segel-, Bade- und Anglerfreuden
am Schwangauer Ufer.

The deep blue of the sky is reflected in the
Forggensee. Now is the best time for the pleasures
of sailing, swimming and fishing afforded by this
lake near Schwangau.

Forggensee: joies de la pêche, de la baignade, des
promenades en voiliers.

Die Tegelbergbahn –
willkommene Aufstiegshilfe ins flora- und
faunareiche Naturschutzgebiet am Tegelberg.
Vom Gipfelkreuz des Branderschrofens überschaut
man den ganzen „Schwanengau" mit seinen
Schlössern, Bergen und Seen.

The Tegelberg funicular is a welcome aid for
reaching the national park on the Tegelberg massif.
From the cross on the Branderschrofen peak it is
possible to overlook the whole of the "Schwangau
district" with its castles, mountains and lakes.

Téléphérique du Tegelberg – Découverte du
panorama magnifique englobant toute la région
autour de Schwangau avec ses châteaux, ses
montagnes et ses lacs.

Hohenschwangau ist internationaler Sight-Seeing-Umschlagplatz. Aber schon gleich neben der Heerstraße des Fremdenverkehrs beginnt die große Ruhe in den Wäldern und an den Ufern des Alpsees.

Hohenschwangau is an international centre of pilgrimage for sightseers. But not far from the tourists' beaten track there is peace and quiet to be found in the forests and by the lakeside of the Alpsee.

Hohenschwangau: centre touristique international, mais aussi hâvre de repos logé au milieu des forêts, sur les rives du lac Alpsee.

Unwegsames Ufer am Bannwaldsee: So finster und streng sein Name klingt, so gastfreundlich gibt sich der See zum Baden und Bootfahren.

Trackless forest edge at the Bannwald-lake; although its name implies sinister connections between the forest and supernatural powers, the lake welcomes swimmers and those who like boatrides.

Bannwaldsee: invitation aux joies de la baignades et des flâneries en bateau!

Dreiklang in Tannengrün, Rostbraun und Himmelblau: der Forggensee, dem man seine Geburt als künstlicher Stausee kaum ansieht.

A harmony of fir green, rust brown and sky blue. The Forggensee, an artificial, man-made lake is hard to spot as such.

Harmonie en trois tons – vert, roux et bleu: c'est le lac Forggensee.

Die unmittelbare Seenähe und der besondere Reiz des Voralpenlandes sind Trümpfe im Angebot des Ferienorts Roßhaupten.

The lake in the immediate vicinity and the special charms of the Lower Alps region are the chief attractions offered by the holiday village of Rosshaupten.

Roßhaupten, niché dans la campagne bavaroise, à proximité des lacs.

Lechbruck –
die alte Tradition lebt nur noch im Denkmal an der Lechbrücke fort. Heute präsentiert sich das ehemalige Flößerdorf längst als begehrter Ferienort mit allem, was dazugehört.

Lechbruck –
the old tradition lives on only in the memorial at the bridge over the River Lech. Nowadays the former timber rafting village presents itself as a desirable place to spend a holiday, with all that this entails.

Lechbruck – charme des anciennes traditions.

Bergfrühling am Hergratsrieder See:
Blühende Löwenzahnwiesen und das fotogene Kapellchen lassen gar manches Fotografenherz höher schlagen.

Spring in the mountains.
At the lake near Hergratsried many a photographer's heart has leapt at the sight of the meadow full of flowering dandelions and the photogenic little chapel.

Printemps sur les bords du lac de Hergratsried. Prairies parsemées de fleurs.

Weiß getüncht, rot bedacht:
Trauchgau und sein Nachbar Buching sind
Ausgangspunkte für das mustergültig erschlossene
Wandergebiet im Halblechtal und rund um die
Kenzenhütte.

Whitewashed, redroofed houses –
Trauchgau and its neighbour Buching are starting
points for hikes in the Halblech valley which has
been mapped out and developed in exemplary
fashion.

Facade blanche, toit rouge flamboyant!
Trauchgau et Buching se présentent à vous comme
points de dèpart de nombreuses promenades dans
la vallée du Halblech.

An der Hochplatte hört das Allgäu endgültig auf.
Hier gibt es die Rolle des Gastgebers an seinen
oberbayerischen Nachbarn weiter.
Und gleichzeitig die Verpflichtung, ein von Gott so
herrlich geschaffenes Land in seiner
Ursprünglichkeit zu bewahren, auf daß es als
paradiesische Ferienlandschaft erhalten bleibe.

The Allgaeu ends at the Hochplatte. Here it passes
on to its neighbour, Upper Bavaria, the privileges
and duties of being host, against a background so
beautifully dreated by God, to visitors from all parts
of the world.

Hochplatte – Haut plateau situé à 2082 m.
C'est la fin de l'Allgäu qui cède ici à son voisin,
la Haute Bavière, à la fois ces droits et ces charges
issus de cette longue tradition synonyme
d'hospitalité, d'accueil et de souci du bien-être du
touriste et du vacancier!